Ejol Nocset

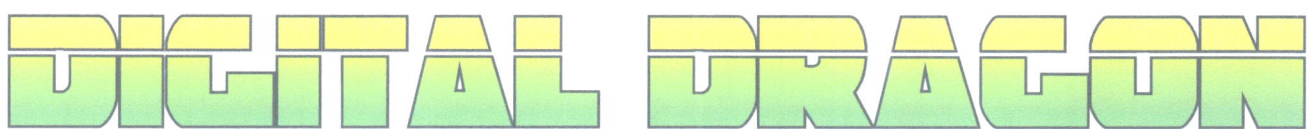

To order additional copies of this book, contact:
Xlibris Corporation
1-888-795-4274
www.Xlibris.com
Orders@Xlibris.com

Prologue

Monday, May 2 2011, 0600 hours local The White House

President of the United States took his copy of an international newspaper off the table after sipping his black coffee. The headline was:

US adopts tougher stance on China

The Pentagon That same time

The commander of Strategic Command USSTRATCOM is a Four-Star Navy Admiral, who is observing the Army Computer Corps and Navy Fleet Cyber Command personnel investigating a malware attacking US Defence Cyberspace. "It may came from China again, Major."

Major Joan Wyle US Air Force Cyber Command, placed her pen next to the keyboard. "Sir, according to our findings, this malware came from China but there are too many decoys."

The USSTRATCOM commander moved closer to the Major's screen and looked at the pictures of possible locations identified by Joint Air Force and Navy cyberspace intelligence personnel.

Beijing Military Museum

Beijing 2

Beijing Global Trade Center

Fujian Fuzhing 1

Fujian Fuzhing 2

Fujian Quanzhou 1

Fujian Quanzhou 2

Fujian Quanzhou 3

Fujian Quanzhou 4

Fujian Quanzhou 5

"The senate may have the right to know but we are still deciding on our actions and policies in South China Sea." The National Security Adviser said.

"I might remind you, Mr President that the senate's analysis and review is not even complete yet. Our review could take several weeks."

Suddenly a man in khaki navy uniform wearing a wireless communications earset opened the door, and saw the White House Chief of Staff standing nearby, and whispered something in his ear. Everybody in the room except Senator Ryan and his assistant Sheena recognized the new comer as Navy Captain Edward Mullen, the Task Force South China Sea senior operations officer who worked temporarily in an office next to the National Security Advisor's office. The White House Chief of Staff just nodded when the President looked at him.

"The meeting is adjourned," the President announced. "Thanks for visit, Senator Ryan."

Fujian Quanzhou 6

Fujian Quanzhou Hotel 1

Fujian Quanzhou Hotel 2

Fujian Xiamen 174 Hospital

Yunnan

Fujian Xiamen In front of Ferry Terminal
to Gulangyu Island

Fujian Xiamen

The Four-Star Navy Admiral stood beside Major Wyle while the Army Computer Corps and Navy Fleet Cyber Command personnel continue working on their consoles to find the malware's origin.

To be continued in Digital Dragon 2…